PROTECTING EARTH'S
WATER
SUPPLY

RON FRIDELL

LERNER PUBLICATIONS COMPANY · MINNEAPOLIS

Text copyright © 2009 by Ron Fridell

Lerner Publications Company
A division of Lerner Publishing Group, Inc.
241 First Avenue North
Minneapolis, MN 55401 U.S.A.

Website address: www.lernerbooks.com

Library of Congress Cataloging-in-Publication Data

Fridell, Ron.
    Protecting earth's water supply / by Ron Fridell.
        p.   cm. — (Saving our living earth)
        Includes bibliographical references and index.
        ISBN 978-0-8225-7557-3 (lib. bdg. : alk. paper)
        1. Water—Pollution. I. Title.
    TD419.F75 2009
    363.739'4—dc22   2007035924

Manufactured in the United States of America
2 3 4 5 6 7 — DP — 14 13 12 11 10 09

CONTENTS

INTRODUCTION

Astronauts enjoy a rare view of our planet: a heavenly body gliding through space wrapped in swirling clouds. For those of us down here on Earth, space travel seems like a dream. But we too are travelers on a different kind of spacecraft, the only planet in the solar system known to harbor life.

When astronauts observe Earth, 70 percent of what they see is water. Water is very important to life on our planet. It makes life possible.

Trillions of living things make their home on planet Earth. Each one is surrounded by its own environment. An environment is made up of elements

Background image: Planet Earth as seen by the crew of the *Apollo 17* spacecraft in 1972. *Right:* A biologist collects insects from a small waterfall. The health of the insects will tell him how healthy the water is.

such as air, water, land, plants, and animals. These elements usually benefit one another. They usually act upon one another in ways that support life. But not always.

Natural events can harm the environment. For example, ash and gases from an erupting volcano can choke the air, killing trees and animals. And people can harm nature too. They build factories that pollute the air. They spill toxins into oceans and lakes, making the water unhealthful.

What can I do to help win this race to protect the environment?

We can't prevent volcanoes or other natural disasters from happening. But we can control the damage humans do to the environment and to our water. Scientists, lawmakers, and business leaders are racing to find new ways to do just that. It's a race against time, though. The human population is growing. And as the number of people rises, so does their potential for doing harm.

What can I do to help win this race to protect the environment? Keep this question in mind as we investigate Earth's most precious resource—water—and our race against time to protect it.

5

CHAPTER ONE

LIQUID GOLD

Every living thing on Earth is made mostly of water. A tomato is 90 percent water. A person is less—about 65 percent. But that's still quite a lot. The average adult body contains 40 to 50 quarts (37–47 liters) of water. Five days is about as long as any of us can survive without water.

We can't grow crops or raise livestock without water either. We use it to produce electrical power and to make everything from paper to steel.

A DROP IN THE BUCKET

Our planet has about 326 million trillion gallons (1,230 million trillion liters) of water. That includes the water traveling through the air in the form of water vapor. (Water vapor is a gas that forms when liquid water evaporates.) Three hundred and twenty-six million trillion gallons may sound like a lot. But 97 percent of this water is salt water. It can't be used for drinking, cooking, or doing laundry.

The remaining 3 percent of Earth's water supply is made up of freshwater. But we can't get at more than two-thirds of that. That's because it's frozen solid. This water is in the ice caps and ice sheets at the North Pole and South Pole.

Less than 1 percent of Earth's total water supply is available for our use.

FIFTY FOOTBALL FIELDS

In some spots, the Antarctic ice sheet at the South Pole is more than 15,000 feet (4,600 meters) thick. How thick is that? Picture fifty football fields minus the end zones stacked up end to end.

Farm fields get a spray from an irrigation system. We need water to grow the foods we eat. Water is essential to the survival of life on Earth.

ONE TINY TEASPOON

Visualize a 1.25-gallon (5-liter) jug of water. Imagine that all of Earth's water is in that jug. Now picture a single teaspoon of that liquid. That teaspoon represents all the freshwater available for all the life on Earth!

H₂O

Each water molecule is made up of two atoms of hydrogen and one atom of oxygen. For that reason, water is also known as H_2O.

Most of this water is groundwater—water that lies under Earth's surface. The rest is surface water. Surface water is the water found in lakes, streams, rivers, and wetlands. More than 99 percent of the water humans use comes from rivers, lakes, and underground sources.

Human demand for freshwater keeps growing. During the last century, the world's human population tripled—and human consumption of water increased by six times! This rising demand increases the stress on Earth's freshwater systems. Most are being damaged or depleted.

Pumps in Florida tap into the groundwater supply to provide drinking water for southern Florida.

WATER ON THE MOVE

Pollutants cause most of the damage to Earth's freshwater supply. Pollutants are substances that make the land, air, or water dirty. How do pollutants get into our freshwater? Most enter during the water cycle.

The water cycle is the continuous movement of water from Earth's surface to the atmosphere and back again. It consists of four stages: evapotranspiration, condensation, precipitation, and collection.

Evapotranspiration is the first stage in the water cycle. During evapotranspiration, water warmed by the sun evaporates from Earth's surface. It turns from an earthbound liquid to an atmospheric gas. About 85 percent of the water that evaporates into Earth's atmosphere comes from oceans. Lakes, rivers, and other bodies of freshwater supply another 5 percent.

The remaining 10 percent enters the atmosphere by transpiration. Transpiration is a process in which plants release water into the air. Plants take in water, along with nutrients, through their roots. During transpiration, some of this water exits through stomata—tiny holes in plants' leaves.

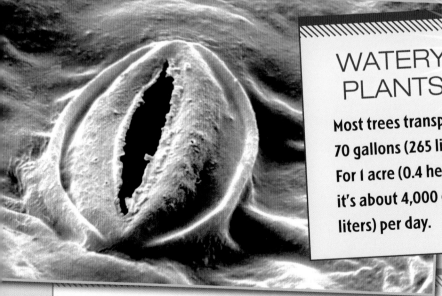

WATERY PLANTS

Most trees transpire about 70 gallons (265 liters) of water a day. For 1 acre (0.4 hectare) of corn, it's about 4,000 gallons (15,000 liters) per day.

Plants release water into the atmosphere through stomata (shown above).

POLLUTED PRECIPITATION

Condensation is the next stage in the cycle. This stage occurs when water vapor in the atmosphere rises. The air gets cold high up in the sky. The cold temperatures cause the water vapor to turn into liquid water droplets. When enough droplets form, they develop into clouds.

MILLIONS OF DROPLETS

It takes millions of water droplets to form a single raindrop.

All of Earth's water gets continuously recycled through the natural processes of evapotranspiration, condensation, precipitation, and collection.

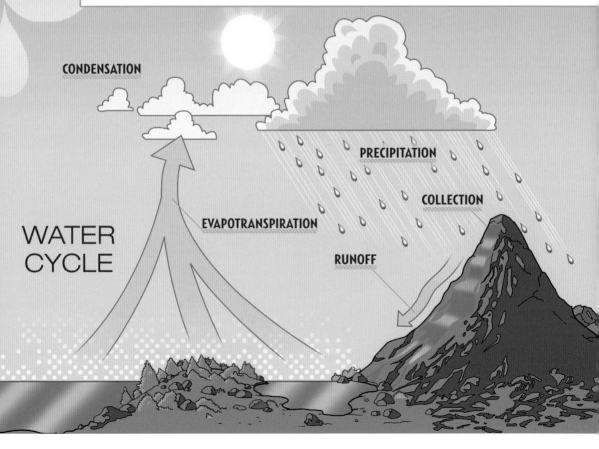

CONDENSATION

PRECIPITATION

COLLECTION

EVAPOTRANSPIRATION

RUNOFF

WATER CYCLE

When so much water has condensed that the air cannot hold it anymore, the third stage in the water cycle occurs—precipitation. Precipitation is rain, sleet, hail, or snow.

Pollution often occurs at the precipitation stage. Precipitation is naturally clean and pure. But power plants and factories release chemical pollutants into the air. Winds carry these pollutants far from their sources. They scatter the pollutants through the atmosphere. As pollutants combine with water vapor droplets, poisonous acids can result.

Rain from clouds polluted with acids is known as acid rain. Acid precipitation also comes in the forms of snow and sleet. Fog can be polluted with acids too.

POISON RAIN

Acid rain can injure trees and pollute lakes and streams worldwide. It can also threaten human health. Children are especially at risk. Acid rain can make asthma and other breathing and lung problems worse.

Acid rain damaged the stone walls of this building in Oxford, England.

THE COLLECTION STAGE

Collection is the final stage of the water cycle. This stage occurs when precipitation hits Earth's surface. In the collection stage, precipitation falls into oceans, lakes, or rivers. Or it falls onto land to become groundwater or runoff. (Runoff is precipitation that hits the ground but eventually flows into bodies of water.)

Pollution is very common at the collection stage. In fact, most of the damage to Earth's freshwater takes place at this point in the water cycle. During collection, pollutants called sediments can get into the water. Sediments are bits of soil, sand, and minerals. They get into freshwater when runoff carries them into lakes, streams, and rivers.

When too many sediments collect in lakes, streams, and rivers, they cloud the water. Sunlight can't shine through the clouded water. This means that sunlight can't reach the many plants that grow beneath the water's surface. The plants can't live without sunlight. They eventually die. And the fish that depend on those plants for food die too.

The biggest producer of sediments is nature itself. But nature is also a great sediment cleaner-upper. Rivers, lakes, wetlands, and other water systems naturally filter and cleanse runoff. They keep themselves in balance.

NATURE OUT OF BALANCE

As humans live their daily lives, they upset this balance.

OLD WATER, NEW WATER

Take a close look at the next glass of water you pick up and be amazed. In your grasp is some of the same liquid that was here 100 million years ago, when dinosaurs roamed Earth.

12

Water in streams and rivers carries with it natural bits of soil, sand, and minerals, as well as human-made pollutants from industry and farming.

Like nature, people pollute freshwater systems. But unlike nature, they do not possess a built-in system for cleansing pollutants. When humans fail to clean up after themselves, freshwater systems suffer.

Most human-made water pollution is caused by chemicals and wastes from agriculture, industry, and sewage treatment. Agriculture is responsible for a great deal of freshwater pollution. Fertilizer, pesticides, and herbicides are used in agriculture. These substances help crops grow. But they also contain strong chemicals. Runoff carries these chemicals into our streams and rivers.

Industry also heavily pollutes our freshwater supply. Currently, industry uses more than one hundred thousand human-made chemicals. And it introduces one thousand new ones into the environment each year.

Acid used in mining operations in California pollutes the surrounding freshwater supply.

Industry uses these chemicals to make products such as electronics and household appliances. Many chemicals are present in the factories where these products are made. The chemicals don't always stay inside the factories. Sometimes they get into the air and soil and wash into our freshwater supply.

Sewage treatment is another common cause of freshwater pollution. Sewage treatment happens at special plants. The plants remove the toxins from sewage water. But sometimes sewage isn't treated properly. Improperly treated sewage can get into runoff or seep into groundwater. This can endanger human health.

THIRSTY FARMS

Chemical pollution isn't the only problem agriculture poses for our freshwater supply. Agriculture is also the biggest freshwater consumer. In fact, agriculture uses about 70 percent of the water available for human use! Most of this water is used for irrigation.

We don't have enough freshwater to waste.

Human-made pollutants have a very destructive impact on our freshwater supply. And we don't have enough freshwater to waste. From out in space, Earth seems to be awash in endless seas of pure blue water. But from up close, it's a different story.

CHAPTER TWO

POLLUTION PROBLEMS

Think of all the places close to home where polluted water could impact your daily life. If you live in a nation in the developed world, such as the United States, the United Kingdom, or Australia, your drinking water comes from either a city water system or a well. Almost anywhere—at home, in a restaurant, at work, or at school—you have access to freshwater. Then there are all the rivers and lakes that people visit to fish, boat, and swim. If those freshwater sources became contaminated, normal life would no longer be normal.

WATER PURIFIED

In the developed world, filtration and chlorination are the techniques used to protect most freshwater supplies from harmful microbes (germs). Filtration and chlorination take place at water treatment plants. Filtration is a process in which water is cleansed. Chlorination is a process in which chlorine is added to water. Chlorine is a powerful germ killer.

In the filtration process, freshwater is filtered down through sand, gravel, or charcoal. Water can flow through tiny spaces in the sand, gravel, or charcoal. But pollutants such as metals cannot. They get stuck. In this way, they are filtered from the water.

In the chlorination process, chlorine—in either gas or liquid form—is added to the water. Chlorine is the disinfectant used to clean swimming pools. It kills harmful microbes.

Left: A family enjoys fishing on a sunny afternoon while bathers swim at the beach.
Below: A water treatment plant

From treatment plants, purified water is sent out through public water systems. This treated water is what you drink from the tap, wash dishes and clothes in, and use to take showers and baths.

WATER CONTAMINATED

Water systems are not foolproof. Purified water can get contaminated on its way to the tap. In some public systems, drinking water and untreated sewage travel in separate pipelines that run side by side. Some of these underground pipes are old and in need of repair. If they spring leaks, raw sewage may seep into drinking water lines. And some rural communities do not have their own public water systems. Instead, people draw their water up from their own wells and send sewage down into septic tanks for treatment. Septic tanks are hollowed-out spaces underground. Bacteria that live in these spaces break down the sewage. Excess liquid drains into the soil. As the liquid trickles through the soil, any remaining impurities decompose, or break down. But poorly constructed or damaged septic systems may allow untreated sewage to seep into well water and contaminate it.

TRY THIS

Water is cleansed naturally as it evaporates from the ground into the air. You can see this process for yourself. Add a teaspoon of hot cocoa mix to a little water in a cup. Leave it for a couple of days. The water will disappear, leaving the cocoa mix behind.

Water systems are not foolproof.

Landfills (places where solid waste is dumped for disposal) can also cause problems for the water supply. Improperly engineered landfills can contaminate groundwater that eventually seeps into wells.

Pollution from landfills, such as this one, can leach into the ground and taint drinking water.

STREAMS AND BEACHES

In September 2006, state water quality experts in northern Pennsylvania did a creek sweep. In a creek sweep, samples are collected from water bodies and tested for contaminants. The experts collected samples from streams that feed into Lake Erie along Presque Isle Bay. This area is a popular recreation spot with eleven scenic beaches. In 2005 and 2006, high levels of the bacteria *Escherichia coli (E. coli)* had caused officials to close one or more of the beaches for days at a time.

  E. coli occurs naturally inside the bodies of warm-blooded animals,

In 2005 and 2006, *E. coli* contaminated the Presque Isle area of Pennsylvania *(shown above)*, leading to the closing of some popular public beaches.

including humans. Without these bacteria in their intestines, people could not digest food. But high levels of *E. coli* in streams means the water is probably contaminated with human or animal waste.

The sweep was conducted after a period of wet weather, so the streams were running high. There didn't seem to be any single source for the *E. coli* outbreak. Experts suspected the cause was runoff and improperly treated sewage from multiple sources. They would have to conduct more studies before they could identify the specific sources. Then they could recommend a course of action to prevent further pollution.

WATERBORNE DISEASES

In Pennsylvania, river water contamination led to just a few beaches being closed. No one became ill, and no one's life was endangered. But things are different in the developing world. In many African countries, millions of poor people live in slums. These crowded areas have no pipes to bring clean water or remove sewage. Instead, human waste is often dumped untreated into streams and rivers. The resulting contamination can seep into wells where people get their drinking water. This can lead to outbreaks of diseases such as cholera.

In August 2006, cholera broke out in Nigeria, a nation in western Africa. About fifteen hundred people were infected, and sixty-eight died. The cause was untreated and contaminated drinking water.

Cholera epidemics are common in northern Nigeria during the rainy season, from June to September. During this time, runoff from storms often spreads contaminated water. The people of northern Nigeria are among the three billion in the developing world who do not have adequate sanitation facilities and the one billion who lack safe drinking water.

ECOSYSTEMS

No matter where on the planet you live—whether it's a rich nation or a poor one—you belong to a wider community than the city or town you call home. You are part of an ecosystem. An ecosystem is a community of living things that depend on one another and their shared environment. The components in an ecosystem are closely interrelated. Whatever happens to one affects the others. A look at the Florida Everglades shows how strongly the human component can affect the other parts of an ecosystem.

The Everglades is a wetland area. Two hundred years ago, the Everglades was known as the River of Grass. It was a flourishing natural landscape that covered an area of 4,000 square miles (10,000 square kilometers). Today the Everglades is half that size. People drained the rest of the land. They turned the drained land into sprawling suburbs and sugar plantations.

Much of the Everglades' water is polluted, largely due to fertilizer runoff from the plantations. Once home to vast flocks of wading birds, the Everglades is now a dying ecosystem. Ninety percent of the birds have vanished. The River of Grass has stopped flowing.

22

WETLANDS TO THE RESCUE

Wetlands such as the Everglades are very beneficial to the environment. They can even help prevent floods and droughts! In times of heavy rain, wetlands can take in and store much of the water that would otherwise flood the land. In times of drought, the water stored in freshwater ecosystems can be pumped out to bring relief to dried-up land and wildlife.

Florida's Everglades National Park *(shown below)* was created to protect what remains of the Everglades' fragile ecosystem. During the wet season, the Everglades' waters drain like a slow-moving flood southward to the Gulf of Mexico.

POLLUTION FACTS

The *Exxon Valdez* spill left an estimated 1,500 miles (2,400 km) of shoreline devastated by oil. The ruined areas included parks, wildlife refuges, and a national forest.

OIL AND WATER

Sometimes a single human disturbance can send an entire ecosystem careening out of balance. In 1989 an oil supertanker called the *Exxon Valdez* struck some rocks in Prince William Sound, Alaska. Almost 11 million gallons (42 million liters) of oil spilled into the water. This was the largest oil spill in U.S. history.

The spill's impact on wildlife was extremely widespread. At least 250,000 seabirds lost their lives. Dozens of other species—such as sea otters, harbor porpoises, sea lions, and whales—also suffered due to the spill. And long after most of the oil was cleaned up, nature was still out of balance. In a 2003

Birds were among the animals hardest hit by the *Exxon Valdez* oil spill near Alaska in 1989.

study, scientists found that some wildlife habitats in Prince William Sound remained contaminated.

The lingering damage affected the ecosystem's human population as well. Two kinds of fish in the area—pink salmon and herring—were unable to reproduce normally. The fishing industry depended on these fish. So fishers began to lose money.

The costs to Exxon, the company that owned the oil tanker, were also steep. As of September 2006, Exxon had paid more than $3 billion in cleanup costs and fines—and the company still hadn't fully paid for all the damage.

Sometimes a single human disturbance can send an entire ecosystem careening out of balance.

EUTROPHICATION AND HYPOXIA

The Mississippi River region is a watershed. A watershed is an area of land that drains into a particular body of water. The Mississippi River region is the third-largest watershed in the world. Some people clear land in the Misissippi region for farming. Or they pave it over to build houses or other buildings. When this happens, erosion results.

Erosion is the gradual wearing away of soil. Without deep plant roots to hold topsoil, the cleared-off soil runs off into the river during rains, becoming sediment. The sediment clogs rivers. Paved areas add to the problem because they don't soak up the water that runs across them. Instead, it all runs off onto the already-soaked land.

Human activities deposit chemicals into this sediment. Some chemicals come from sewage treatment plants and fertilized suburban lawns. But most come

Low levels of oxygen in water bodies can lead to the death of large numbers of fish.

26

from farm fields. Farmers spread lots of fertilizer on their fields. The fertilizer contains nitrogen and phosphorus. Nitrogen and phosphorus are nutrients. When they get into bodies of water, they cause tons of algae to grow.

Eventually, the algae dies. As it dies, it sinks to the bottom of water bodies and decomposes. This process consumes lots of oxygen. Fish and other aquatic animals need this oxygen to live. The name for this deadly process is eutrophication. The resulting condition—oxygen-poor water—is called hypoxia.

DEAD ZONES

A huge area suffering from eutrophication and hypoxia is located off Louisiana's Gulf coast. This stretch of water is the size of the state of New Jersey. Since the 1970s, marine biologists have been finding such areas along coastlines around the planet. Most are near the mouths of rivers that pour polluted runoff into the ocean. These damaged areas are known as dead zones.

ACCUMULATED CONSEQUENCES

Some ocean water pollutants enter the bodies of fish and seabirds and remain there. Scientists call this process bioaccumulation. Mercury is one pollutant that can bioaccumulate in fish. Bioaccumulation of mercury harms the fish. It also harms the health of people who eat the fish.

Whether it's close to home or far away, pollution affects nearly all the water on Earth. Every living thing—including humans—belongs to an ecosystem that relies on freshwater or ocean water. Water pollution is becoming a more pressing challenge with each passing day. What are we doing to meet this challenge?

TRAVELING MERCURY

The Arctic is one of the most remote places on Earth. Yet this region is a global hotspot for mercury. It arrives by air and water from factories that release it in the United States. The animals of the Arctic are severely affected by mercury. In fact, Arctic animals have higher levels of mercury than animals anywhere else in the world.

27

CHAPTER THREE

POLLUTION SOLUTIONS

In 1962 biologist Rachel Carson wrote a groundbreaking book. The book is called *Silent Spring*. It describes the damage that human-made chemicals do to ecosystems. *Silent Spring* helped change the way people looked at pollution. Before it was published, many people saw pollution as a natural consequence of human progress. Carson's book changed that point of view. *Silent Spring* helped launch environmentalism—a social movement that sees pollution as a preventable crime against nature.

NEW LAWS

In the 1960s, millions of people began speaking out for the environment. They demanded new laws to control human activities harmful to nature. The government responded. In 1969 the U.S. Congress passed the National Environmental Policy Act (NEPA). NEPA made the government responsible for protecting the environment.

28

In 1970 Congress created the U.S. Environmental Protection Agency (EPA). The EPA would set and enforce environmental standards to ensure that all Americans enjoyed safe and healthful surroundings.

SILENT SPRING

Silent Spring focuses on the bioaccumulation of pesticides in wildlife. It discusses the toll pesticides take on many animals, particularly birds. The title refers to what spring would be like if there were no more songbirds.

On April 22, 1970, junior high school students in Kirkwood, Missouri, protest against automobile pollution in honor of Earth Day.

Four years later, legislators passed the Safe Drinking Water Act (SDWA). Under the SDWA, the EPA regulates contaminants such as arsenic, radium, and lead. This means that the government sets maximum allowable levels for these contaminants in drinking water. These regulations help keep drinking water safe from pollution.

WASTEWATER AND ACID RAIN

The government passed laws to protect ecosystems from wastewater pollution as well. The Federal Water Pollution Control Act (FWPCA) of 1972 set strict standards for city and industrial wastewater treatment. It also required industrial plants to install up-to-date pollution-control technologies.

The FWPCA has helped reduce the amount of harmful pollutants released into harbors of cities such as New York, San Diego, and Los Angeles. As a result, oxygen levels are higher in the harbor waters. The harbor ecosystems are healthier than they once were.

Another law—the 1990 Clean Air Act—has helped reduce acid rain pollution. The Clean Air Act regulates the amount of pollutants that power plants and factories can release. Damage from acid rain has been especially destructive in the eastern United States. Thanks to the Clean Air Act, lakes and streams in this region are showing improvements.

Regulations help keep drinking water safe from pollution.

The Florida panther once lived in parts of Arkansas, Louisiana, Mississippi, Alabama, Georgia, Tennessee, and South Carolina. This animal now lives only in the Florida Everglades.

ENDANGERED PANTHERS

Laws go a long way in the quest to protect our planet. But lawmakers aren't the only ones involved in conservation efforts. Many environmental groups are taking action too. The National Wildlife Federation (NWF) is one such group.

In 2000 the NWF turned its attention to the Florida panther. The Florida panther is one of the world's rarest mammals. It lives only in the wetlands of the Florida Everglades. The panthers' Everglades habitat already had been reduced to half its original size. Now it was in danger of shrinking even more. The threat came from plans set in place by the U.S. Army Corps of Engineers. This agency plans and carries out construction projects around rivers and wetlands. In 2000 the corps announced a plan to mine limestone on 5,200 acres (2,100 hectares) of panther habitat in the Everglades.

The Endangered Species Act of 1973 requires that a list be kept of plants and animals in danger of extinction. It also requires protection for all plants and animals on the list. The Florida panther was on the list. The NWF and other environmental groups took the corps to court to stop the mining. The environmentalists won their case. The corps' mining project was canceled.

AN AMAZING EXPERIMENT

The NWF has professional experience, money, and thousands of members. But what about individuals with little money or experience? Can such people really make a difference? Zachary Bjornson-Hooper, a student from Alamo, California, has proven that they can.

During a plane trip in 2002, Zachary heard a flight attendant talking about the taste of drinking water on the plane. Her words gave Zachary an idea. He needed to plan a science project, and he also had a trip to Australia coming up. He decided to combine the two and investigate the quality of airline tap water. Airlines usually serve bottled water. When that runs out, they use water from onboard tanks. It's the same water that runs out of faucets in the bathrooms. According to the airlines, this water was supposed to be safe to drink. But was it?

During his trip, Zachary collected samples of airline water. When he got home, he examined the samples through a microscope. What he saw was alarming. Bacteria were growing like mad!

Not many science projects get nationwide attention. Zachary's did. Reporters from the *Wall Street Journal* responded to Zachary's experiment by launching an investigation of their own. They sampled water on long flights and short flights to different cities on different airlines. Scientists

analyzed the reporters' samples. They found that some were fine—but others contained harmful bacteria. Water from one flight was contaminated by *Salmonella* bacteria. This bacteria can cause serious illness. A sample from another flight contained aquatic insect eggs that hatched into larvae.

As a result of Zachary's science project, laws were changed nationwide. Tap water supplies on U.S. aircraft now must go through thorough health inspections.

TECHNOLOGY TO THE RESCUE

Laws are one solution to pollution. Other solutions involve replacing existing technologies with cleaner ones. Still others aim to create products and technologies to help clean up polluted waters.

Technology has helped us make great strides in reducing pollution from power plants. Power plants need a constant supply of freshwater to cool and clean their equipment. To meet this need, some plants take in streams of freshwater from water bodies. Power plants pull the streams of water in at

33

one end and eventually discharge, or release, them at the other. Plants that use water in this way are known as open-loop plants.

Open-loop plants pose many risks to aquatic life. When they take in streams of freshwater, they also take in fish and animals. This kills the fish and animals. And plants chlorinate and heat the water they take in. When they discharge the chlorinated, heated water, unhealthful chemicals get into water bodies.

Technology provides a better way for power plants to use water. It is based on nature itself. It's called a closed-loop system. In a closed-loop system, power plants use a single supply of water over and over again. They recycle water—just as nature does in the

SMITHA'S MISSION

Fourteen-year-old Smitha Ramakrishna of Chandler, Arizona, has also joined the mission to uncover pollution solutions. In 2003 Smitha and her parents visited India. Smitha was concerned to see so many children attending schools without clean water.

When Smitha got home, she volunteered to help supply this need. Smitha recruited volunteers to help raise money. Two walk-a-thons brought in four thousand dollars for the cause. The money went toward purchasing a water treatment system for the schoolchildren.

More than three thousand young people benefit from Smitha's efforts—and Smitha's ambitions did not stop there. In 2006 Smitha traveled to Mexico to let people from all over the world know about her work. She presented her project to the Children's World Water Forum. At this meeting, people from many countries gather to discuss solutions to water-related problems.

Power plants can pose grave risks to water bodies.

35

water cycle. Closed-loop systems are safer for plants and animals. And they don't discharge polluted water into water bodies. They provide an environmentally responsible way for power plants to clean and maintain their equipment.

DUMMIES AND SCARE CANS

How do you clean up a gigantic oil spill at sea? It's best to pick up the oil before it drifts. But more often than not, the spill is in a remote area, or the seas are very rough. By the time cleanup crews arrive, the oil has already spread.

If spilled oil is not taken care of right away, it will eventually reach shore. Then an army of workers must clean the shoreline by hand. To begin with, they use low- and high-pressure water hoses and vacuum trucks. Spongy materials that can soak up oil—called sorbents—are used in the final stages of cleanup. Sometimes oil-soaked sand and gravel must be taken away and cleaned up, then put back in place.

Seabirds and other animals that are covered with oil must be cleaned as well. They are washed by human hands in gentle dishwashing liquid. Meanwhile, workers leave high-tech versions of scarecrows at the site of the spill to keep other birds from landing in the mess. Floating dummies are anchored in shallow water, and helium-filled balloons are tethered to the shoreline.

DID YOU KNOW?

Forty percent of America's rivers are too polluted for fishing, swimming, or the survival of aquatic life.

A cormorant gets its feathers cleaned after the 1989 *Exxon Valdez* oil spill near Alaska.

Oil spilled near Toledo, Oregon, in 2001 spread through the water in spite of workers' efforts to contain it.

Propane scare cans—devices that give out loud popping noises—are also set in shallow water.

FENCES AND CHEMICALS

Cleaning up shoreline habitats can take decades, as in the case of the *Exxon Valdez* oil spill. How can a spill be cleaned up quickly, before it reaches shore?

Oil tankers carry "spill kits" on board. Spill kits include sorbent pads made of oil-attracting material. They are dabbed in the oil and then squeezed out on board the ship. Kits also contain bales of hay and pitchforks. The hay absorbs and holds the oil. The pitchforks are used to pull up tarlike layers of thickened oil.

Another cleanup method uses booms. Booms are floating fences. The ship's crew lays them out to keep the oil away from the shore. Then they use oil-absorbent plastic ropes and vacuum machines to skim the surface of the water and collect the oil.

Cleaning up shoreline habitats can take decades.

37

Dispersants are one more option. These chemicals break down the oil. They transform it into a substance that is less harmful to aquatic life. Dispersants can be applied in rough seas where other methods may not work.

NEW INVENTIONS

Coral reefs are fast disappearing from the planet, due in large part to pollution. The Reef Ball Foundation is an organization with a mission to restore coral reef systems around the world.

A reef ball is a module—or section—of artificial reef. It is made of special concrete that looks like a natural reef. It can be as small as a basketball or as big as a car. The Reef Ball Foundation sinks reef balls into ocean water off coastlines. On top of them, the foundation plants pieces of broken coral damaged by storms. The pieces contain living coral. The foundation also places sponges, sea squirts, and other aquatic life on the reef balls. Eventually, these modules grow into natural coral reefs.

The foundation's director, Doug Hollingsworth, says, "We've got everything that wants to be on a coral reef growing on the Reef Balls, and the fish move in right away. As soon as the Reef Balls hit the bottom, 'bam!' fish move inside, and the other stuff begins to grow on them."

THE GREAT BARRIER REEF

Australia's Great Barrier Reef is the largest coral reef in the world. It is home to an amazing variety of animals, including dolphins, whales, turtles, and dugongs— huge marine mammals that look a lot like manatees. Many people like to visit the Great Barrier Reef. But this fragile ecosystem is in danger. Pollution, overfishing, and poor water quality have put this remarkable reef at risk.

38

A reef ball provides a comfortable home for coral animals off the coast of Indonesia.

Black Sea fishers fill their net with jellyfish in 2003.

The foundation has built thirty-five hundred reefs consisting of more than half a million reef balls in fifty countries around the world.

CUTTING BACK

The most obvious solution for pollution problems is to cut back on the source: the pollutants themselves. In the case of dead zones, that means cutting back on the amount of fertilizer used on farm fields. The less fertilizer runoff there is pouring into oceans, the less phosphorus and nitrogen there is to cause eutrophication of ocean water.

Dead zones are reversible. The proof is in the Black Sea. This sea between Europe and Asia used to be the world's largest dead zone. Heavy fertilizer runoff from farms in Eastern Europe had caused extensive eutrophication.

During the 1980s, eutrophication killed the seafloor's aquatic ecosystem, along with the Black Sea's fishing industry.

Even severe water pollution
damage can be repaired.

Then came the breakup of the Soviet Union. The Soviet Union was a very large Eastern European nation. It split up into many different countries in 1991. After the Soviet Union broke apart, many who used to live there became very poor. Many farmers who used to buy fertilizer for their crops could no longer afford it. As a result, much less fertilizer made its way into the Black Sea. In just a decade, the dead zone disappeared. Fish returned to the Black Sea. The area's fishing industry came back to life.

Of course, this pollution solution was not voluntary. The polluting fertilizer was cut back for economic reasons, not environmental concerns. But the Black Sea revival is a hopeful sign. It shows that even severe water pollution damage can be repaired.

CONSERVATION SOLUTIONS

Laws and technology can help a great deal in the effort to control water pollution. But pollution is only half the problem. The other half is preserving Earth's water supply. There is only so much freshwater to go around. With Earth's population on the rise, the demand for freshwater keeps growing. Since we can't increase the supply to meet the growing demand, we must somehow make do with less freshwater per person as time moves on.

There is only so much freshwater to go around.

Does this mean the human race is destined to run out of water one day? Not if we take into account how much of this life-giving liquid we waste and do what we can to preserve it.

WHY NOT GRAY WATER?

Gray water is the liquid drained from clothes washers, sinks, and showers. It does not include water from toilets. (That liquid is called black water.) Using gray water in place of freshwater is a key strategy for effective water conservation.

Gray water can replace freshwater for many uses. Car washes are beginning to use gray water instead of freshwater. Gray water is also being used to water golf courses and playing fields.

In some states, homeowners can set up their own gray water recycling systems.

Left: A University of Arizona research technician points out that there is no difference between grass watered with gray water and grass watered with treated water. *Below:* A collection of greenery watered with gray water thrives in a sunny window.

MORE ON THE WAY

Experts predict that by the year 2030, Earth's human population will increase by 1.7 billion.

Instead of going to a treatment plant or septic system, indoor gray water is recycled for outdoor use. People use it to wash cars and water lawns.

Gray water recycling systems typically save homeowners 15 to 50 percent on water costs. This water conservation trend is picking up steam in states such as Texas, Arizona, and New Mexico. In these places, frequent droughts can lead to freshwater shortages.

GRAY WATER OUTLAWS

Some people take gray water use too far. Public officials get complaints about people who run hoses from their washing machines outside to water their plants. The complaints are from next-door neighbors whose yards get flooded!

44

AGGRESSIVE CONSERVATION

Experts say that water conservation demands a change in attitude. Effective conservation means not waiting for an emergency to act. It means planning for the future.

City officials in Boston, Massachusetts, have adopted this attitude, known as aggressive conservation. In the 1980s, officials in the Boston metropolitan area were looking ahead. In years to come, as the area's population grew, demand for water was expected to exceed supply. How could this problem be addressed before it became an emergency?

The simplest solution was to draw more water from the Connecticut River. But citizens were against that plan. They were concerned about damage to the river's ecosystem. City officials rethought their options. They came up with a different plan. Instead of drawing more water from the river, why not

The Connecticut River winds through Massachusetts between towering stands of trees.

make better use of the water they were drawing now?

Boston started an aggressive conservation program in 1987. It focused on eliminating waste in the city's water systems. It included finding and repairing leaks in water pipes, outfitting 370,000 homes with more efficient plumbing, and educating the public about water conservation.

How well did the program work? Between 1987 and 2004, water use in the Boston area fell 31 percent. And it wasn't because people were using less water. Instead, it was because they were *wasting* less. The Boston example shows that cities can provide drinking water for growing populations without damaging ecosystems.

46

A drip-style irrigation system waters grapevines in Napa Valley, California.

DRIP . . . DRIP . . . DRIP

Rural irrigation systems waste water too. Most of Earth's freshwater is used for agriculture—but only about half of that water actually reaches the crops. That's because most irrigation systems take a top-down approach. They spray water outward so it falls onto crops from above, haphazardly, like rain. A great deal of water is lost to evaporation and runoff before plants have a chance to absorb it.

What happens when farmers use a bottom-up approach? Instead of water shooting out in large, pressurized quantities, what if it gently drips into the soil? Drip-style irrigation sends water through holes in tubing laid at ground level. The water is applied in controlled amounts directly to the roots, where plants naturally absorb it. This way, much less water is lost to evaporation or runoff.

Cost is another drip irrigation plus. Drip irrigation tubing is cheaper and easier to install than top-down systems. In India, where one in five people do not get enough to eat, drip systems offer new hope. An inexpensive storage tank or a nearby stream sends water through drip tubing to small plots of vegetables and grains. For a farm family in India, these crops can mean a way out of malnourishment and poverty.

USED-UP AQUIFERS

Aquifers are natural underground formations of sand, soil, gravel, or rock. They collect and store groundwater. Aquifers are a good source of freshwater. But people are using up all the water in aquifers. They use machines to drill into the ground and pump the water out.

Ninety-five percent of U.S. freshwater supplies are located underground. As people take water out of aquifers, water tables drop. The water table is the top of the groundwater—the highest level at which the soil is fully saturated with water. The lower the water table, the deeper down machines must drill to reach water that can be pumped out.

Some aquifers get used up faster than others. The Ogallala Aquifer—which stretches from Texas to South Dakota—provides 20 percent of the water used to irrigate U.S. farmland. Water is being taken from the aquifer more quickly than nature can recharge it. Some estimates predict that the Ogallala will be entirely depleted in twenty-five years unless aggressive conservation measures are taken.

FROM DESERT TO BREADBASKET

The Ogallala area was once known as the Great American Desert. That was before settlers started farming the land in the 1880s. They used water from aquifers to irrigate fields of wheat and other crops. Soon the area was renamed the nation's breadbasket.

SETTING LIMITS

People are using different tactics to control aquifer depletion.

The Texas blind salamander cannot survive without a clean supply of water from the Edwards Aquifer.

Sometimes these tactics involve endangered species. The Texas blind salamander and the fountain darter are endangered aquatic animals. They live only in the Edwards Plateau region of Texas. This area gets most of its water supply from the Edwards Aquifer. Heavy pumping of the Edwards Aquifer had reduced river flows to dangerous levels in the habitats of these rare animals.

An environmental group called the Sierra Club took action. It filed a lawsuit on behalf of the Texas blind salamander and the fountain darter. The Sierra Club won the lawsuit. The Texas state legislature was forced to limit how much water could be pumped from the aquifer.

Tiered pricing is another tactic. Some water companies use tiered pricing. This means that they set the prices for water in stair-step fashion. Customers who use the most water have to pay the most. And customers who use the least get to pay the least. Tiered pricing encourages farmers, factory owners, and city dwellers to use less water.

FRESHWATER AROUND THE WORLD

Many people around the world lack fresh drinking water. Why? One reason is shortages in water supply. There would be enough water on Earth to meet everyone's needs if only it were distributed evenly.

Uneven water distribution leads to water shortages in many parts of the world. Some places, such as Ontario, Canada *(shown above),* have vast supplies of water. Others have scant water supplies.

But some nations have more water than they know what do with. Canada, for example, has less than 1 percent of the world's population, but it enjoys 20 percent of the world's available freshwater. Canada has large stretches of lakes and rivers. So Canadians have more freshwater than they could ever use.

The situation is reversed in developing nations. China has 20 percent of the world's people. But it has only 7 percent of the world's freshwater supply. And things are even worse in the Middle East. There, 5 percent of the world's population has only 1 percent of the world's freshwater. Most of the world's population growth in years to come will be in developing nations such as India, China, and Saudi Arabia. That means the strain on their water resources will grow too.

What about rich nations? Their populations will not increase as fast as those of poorer nations. But each year, people in developed nations use more water per person. This means their water needs will also keep growing.

With population and per-person needs rising everywhere, water will become scarcer and scarcer. What steps can we take to ease the strain to come?

RAINWATER HARVESTING

The use of drip irrigation already is helping conserve freshwater. And so is rainwater harvesting. Rainwater harvesting is an old practice. People harvested rainwater thousands of years ago in Africa, the Middle East, Asia, Central America, and South America. In these parts of the world, rain tends to fall heavily during a few months of the year—and the rest of the year, there is drought. The rainy season is known as the monsoon. How can monsoon rains be harvested and stored for use during the dry season?

One thousand years ago, the Maya (a group of people from the Yucatán region of Mexico) developed technology to address this need. Their tradition of rainwater harvesting depended on reservoirs and cisterns, special holding

An underground Mayan water tank can be seen in the ancient Mayan city of Tikal, Guatemala.

areas for storing water. The Maya dug reservoirs in valleys. Some of them were 330 feet (100 m) across. Rainwater running down hills into the valleys collected in the reservoirs. During the dry season, farmers used the collected water to irrigate fruit trees and crops.

For drinking water, the Maya used cisterns. They dug these storage tanks into the ground at the bottom of hills. They cleared the land above them to help funnel runoff into the cisterns. Each one could hold up to 12,000 gallons (45,000 liters) of harvested rainwater.

51

A YOUNG HERO

Use of rainwater harvesting in India can go a long way toward supplying people with the water they need. In southwestern India, monsoon rains come for three or four months each year. During the period of drought that follows, freshwater can become dangerously scarce.

Anagha Ann Gopakumar, of Aluva, India, made it her mission to help farmers meet their water needs during the dry season. To gather knowledge, Anagha read books, looked at websites, and talked with her grandparents about how rainwater was harvested in the past.

Anagha used what she learned to develop her own rainwater harvesting system. She set up the system on her family's house. Bamboo gutters funneled rainwater into a container. Pebbles and charcoal in the container

Anagha Ann Gopakumar created a rainwater harvesting system to help supply water to neighboring farmers.

helped to filter the water. Below that, a pipe ran from the container to a well.

When monsoon rains began, Anagha's harvesting system was ready. By the time monsoon season ended, Angha had accomplished her mission. In the well was water for the irrigation needs of local farmers.

Anagha won an International Young Eco-Hero Award for her achievement. This award recognizes young people ages eight to sixteen for their environmental achievements. When she won the award in 2006, Anagha was only ten years old.

WATER FROM AIR

Anagha's harvesting system was based on ideas from ancient civilizations. The atmospheric water generator (AWG) is based on modern science. This machine literally produces water out of thin air.

The AWG gathers humidity from the surrounding air to produce drinking water. When air is passed through a cooled metal coil, water vapor condenses out of it. The condensed water is collected for use.

Many technologies that people use in everyday life were first developed for the military. AWG technology was a project of DARPA, the Pentagon's Defense Advanced Research Projects Agency. DARPA was looking for ways to supply freshwater to U.S. troops stationed in the desert.

The AWG is being marketed to countries where water is scarce. It can run on electric or solar power. Operating costs are low. Using the AWG to produce 0.26 gallon (1 liter) of water costs just three to six cents.

52

Fog-collecting nets in South Africa provide a local village with much-needed freshwater.

The AWG can operate with the humidity as low as 14 percent. The higher the humidity, the more water it produces. In very humid air, the machine can turn out as many as 600 gallons (2,300 liters) of water a day.

WATER FROM FOG

In some dry places, freshwater can be collected from fog. Picture big sections of mesh fabric stretched between wooden poles. The sections are mounted above troughs in the ground. Now picture morning fog hitting the mesh and condensing. Droplets form and then slide down into the collecting troughs below.

With enough fog and enough mesh, a surprising amount of water can be collected—even in dry places such as the coast of Chile. In 1992, along a ridge on El Tofo Mountain in northern Chile, people set up ninety-four fog collectors. They piped the collected water to the nearby coastal village of Chungungo. On average, 4,000 gallons (15,000 liters) of water a day were piped to the village. In the past, water had been scarce in Chungungo. Now everyone has plenty.

FRESHWATER FROM SALT WATER

Wouldn't you just love a nice, big, ice-cold glass of seawater? No, you would not. We humans can't drink salt water, also known as saline water. Drinking it on a regular basis would soon cause death from dehydration.

There is a truly endless supply of saline water, though. The world's oceans are full of it. If only we could get rid of that salt and the other harmful substances dissolved in it—and we can! Saline water can be made into freshwater in a process called desalination.

The goal of desalination is simple: remove enough salt to make seawater drinkable. Seawater contains about 35,000 parts per million of dissolved salts. Reduce that amount to less than 1,000 parts per million, and you have freshwater.

Like rainwater harvesting, desalination began in ancient times. The armies of Roman leader Julius Caesar used it more than two thousand years ago. The basic process is the same one nature uses in the water cycle. Heated water evaporates, leaving behind salt and other impurities. As the distilled, or purified, water vapor rises, it runs into cooler air and condenses to form precipitation. Like nature, Caesar's armies relied on solar energy to evaporate the salt water.

54

SEE FOR YOURSELF

You can see desalination at work for yourself. Set a dish of salty water out in the sun, and put a clear cover on it. After a while, you'll see drops of water that have condensed on the inside of the cover.

An onlooker stands before a large desalination plant in the Middle East.

SPEEDING UP NATURE

Today most desalination happens at desalination plants. And the process goes much faster than it did in ancient times. Desalination plants burn fuel to create intense heat. The heat is applied to thin sprays of water. The water evaporates instantly. This method is called flash distillation.

More than two thousand desalination plants worldwide use flash distillation. Other plants use a newer method called reverse osmosis. In reverse osmosis, pressure is applied to salt water. The pressure forces the salt water through a membrane, or special screen. The salt gets stuck in the membrane. Only pure water passes through.

DID YOU KNOW?

Desalination plants are most common in the Middle East and the Caribbean Islands. Desalination is also used aboard ships and submarines.

Desalination may one day be the best answer to our water scarcity problems. But right now, the technology is extremely expensive. It costs five to ten times as much to produce drinkable water from ocean water as from sources such as gray water.

There are still no magic answers to the planet's water pollution and scarcity problems. The race against time continues.

CHAPTER FIVE

INTO THE FUTURE

What new technologies are scientists pursuing to protect and conserve Earth's water in the future? To begin with, they are looking for new technology to clean or distribute water. One solution could come from one of the lightest solid substances known to science: aerogels. These absorbent, foamlike materials weigh just a bit more than air. That's because they're nearly 99 percent air. Yet aerogels are strong. They can support many times their own weight.

Aerogels are also versatile. They make great insulators. The National Aeronautics and Space Administration (NASA) used them to insulate *Sojourner*, a robot designed to explore Mars. NASA also uses them to capture space dust and bring it back to Earth for study. Aerogels are water repellent as well. Blankets chemically treated with aerogels keep campers warm and dry.

But what have aerogels got to do with water pollution? A team of scientists in California has developed what they call hydrophobic aerogels. *Hydrophobic* means "water-repelling." Dropped into an oil-water mixture, hydrophobic aerogels take in only the oil. Hydrophobic aerogels can absorb four to sixteen times their weight in oil. The scientists hope to one day develop super-absorbent hydrophobic aerogels that can hold even more oil. They could become a powerful new technology to combat oil spills.

NASA used this aerogel sample to collect comet dust in a 1999 space mission.

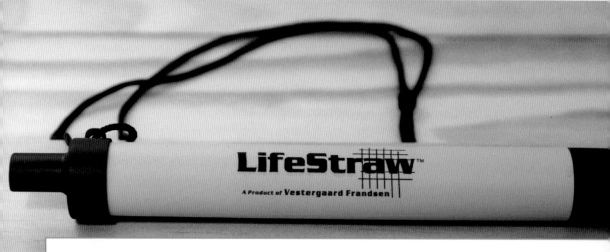

The LifeStraw water purifier provides a way for people in need to get drinking water that is free of dangerous contaminants.

LIFESTRAW

58

In the developing world, about six thousand people die each day from waterborne diseases. The main reason is drinking water contaminated with waste. Poor nations without sewage or water treatment systems need new, inexpensive ways to purify this contaminated water for drinking.

LifeStraw is a technology that addresses that need. This sturdy straw is made of plastic. It looks something like a flute. The user holds a cup of water with one hand and the LifeStraw with the other. As the user sucks up water through the LifeStraw, it travels through filters and a special chamber. In the process, the bacteria responsible for waterborne diseases are killed.

LifeStraw was created by Danish inventor Torben Vestergaard Frandsen. The product could be a lifesaver. The only problem with LifeStraw is the cost. Each straw costs three dollars and fifty cents. That may not sound like very much. But most people in countries that lack clean water earn less than one dollar a day. To many of them, LifeStraw is a very expensive item.

DISTRIBUTING WATER

Distribution of limited water resources is a big problem. How can we transport water to the people who need it most? Governments and businesses are looking into efficient, inexpensive ways to move water from place to place.

Pipelines are one way to move water. Plans are under way to build pipelines from Scotland, where water is plentiful, to England, where water is getting scarce. Plans are also in the works to build pipes from Turkey to central Europe and the Middle East.

SPARKLING BUT DANGEROUS

Picture yourself kneeling beside a sparkling mountain stream. You plunge your hands into the cool, crystal-clear water and lift them to your face. But wait. Even the most remote mountain stream may well contain *Giardia* or coliform bacteria. These bacteria come from the feces of wild animals. They could give you stomach cramps, diarrhea, or worse. Boil, filter, or disinfect that cool, clear water before you taste it.

Distribution of limited water resources is a big problem.

Ships are another way to get water where it needs to go. Companies ship water in large quantities by sea, using floating bags. The Nordic Water Supply company floats freshwater from Turkey to the island of Cyprus in 5-million-gallon (19-million-liter) bags.

Then there is bottled water. Bottled water is already being transported all around the world. The governments of some developing nations may decide not to build tap water systems at all. Instead, they may rely on businesses that sell bottled water cheaply. China is already moving in this direction. Between 1997 and 2002, their use of bottled water increased by 400 percent.

HERE COME THE ICEBERGS!

One outlandish idea for transporting freshwater involves the icebergs at the North Pole and South Pole. Two-thirds of Earth's water lies at the poles—yet no one has been able to access it. But Australian scientist Patrick Quilty has a plan. He believes the icebergs could be towed to Africa by ship.

In Quilty's plan, the icebergs would be wrapped in plastic bags—much like the bags used for towing water. The bags would be big enough to hold an iceberg. They would also be strong, since ice is very heavy.

Would Quilty's plan really be possible? The average iceberg is about the size of a fifteen-story building and could weigh millions of tons. But Quilty has plotted out a route from Antarctica to northeast Africa where ocean currents would supply most of the energy needed for transport.

CONSUMER FACT

At least 25 percent of bottled water starts out as plain tap water. Experts say that smart advertising is the main reason bottled water sells so well. Bottled water costs far more than tap water, isn't necessarily cleaner or safer than tap water, and can severely deplete water supplies in places where it is bottled. Plastic water bottles also cause pollution when they get into the environment. Only some of these bottles are recycled. The rest end up in landfills.

60

Terry Spragg, a businessman from California, stands on a giant bag meant for transporting water. Spragg dreams of using water-transport bags to deliver water to Palestinians and Israelis.

Icebergs have been towed before, but not very far. Oil companies must sometimes move icebergs so they can drill for oil that lies under the ocean. The oil companies run a towline around an iceberg, lassoing it. Then a ship pulls it a short distance. But no one has ever put a long-distance plan like Quilty's into action—yet.

All these present and future plans and technologies to cleanse and conserve Earth's water involve scientists, engineers, corporations, and governments. But what about you? What can you do to help?

SPRAGG BAGS

California businessman Terry Spragg wants to use water to make the world a more peaceful place. He thinks the U.S. government should fill giant sacks with water and ship them to the Palestinians and the Israelis. The Palestinians and the Israelis have been involved in a conflict for many years. Spragg thinks the U.S. government could convince them to make peace if it sent them a gift of water.

The government has not tried Spragg's idea—but Spragg is convinced it could work. He even has a name picked out for his water-filled sacks: Spragg Bags!

GOING GREEN

Here are some tips to help get you started in the fight to save Earth's water supply. These small steps can go a long way in the effort to protect and conserve our world's most precious resource.

- **Clean up after your pets.**
  Pet waste contains nutrients and bacteria that can contaminate surface water.

- **Buy detergents and cleaners that are low in phosphorus. And try to use natural shampoos, conditioners, and body washes.**
  This will help reduce the amount of nutrients and pollutants that are discharged into lakes, streams, and coastal waters.

- **Leave lawn clippings on your lawn.**
  When grass is mowed, many clippings are left behind. It's best to leave them there. That way, nutrients in the clippings are recycled and less yard waste goes to landfills.

- **Control runoff from rainstorms.**
  Install gravel trenches along driveways or patios to collect water and allow it to filter into the ground.

You can save plenty of water at home by simply turning off the faucet while you brush your teeth.

- **Instead of buying new clothing, try making new styles with the clothing you have. Or try exchanging clothing with your friends.** Lots of clothing is made of cotton—and many pesticides are used to grow cotton. Runoff can carry chemicals from pesticides into our water supply. By coming up with new styles using clothing you already own, you'll help reduce the impact your clothing choices have on planet Earth.

63

- **Don't let water go to waste in your home.**
  Here are some ideas for you and your family to try:
  - Run dishwashers and clothes washers only when they are fully loaded.
  - Take short showers instead of baths.
  - Turn off the water while brushing your teeth.
  - Don't let warm-up water go down the drain. As you wait for hot water to come down the pipes, catch the flow in a watering can. Use it later to water your garden.
  - Water your lawn only when it needs it. Step on your grass. If it springs back when you lift your foot, it doesn't need water.
  - When you water your lawn or garden, use slow watering techniques such as trickle irrigation or soaker hoses.

GOING GREEN

Writing to government leaders is a great way to communicate your concern about Earth's water supply. Anyone can send a letter to a senator or representative. Not sure how to get started? Read on for a few helpful hints.

- **Choose a particular issue to write about.**
  Is there a polluted lake near your home? Is runoff a problem in your community? Keep your letter focused by zeroing in on a specific concern.

- **Explain why the issue matters to you.**
  Write from your heart. Your letter doesn't have to be long or complicated. Just explain how you feel and use your own words.

- **Be courteous.**
  Use respectful language at all times. And if you get a response from your legislator, you can follow up with a thank-you letter. That will show your legislator how much you value his or her time. It will also help bring more attention to your cause.

- **Make sure to spell your legislators' names and addresses correctly.**
  Legislators may not take your letter seriously if their names are misspelled. And your letter may not reach them at all if it isn't addressed correctly. So be sure to look your legislators' names up on the Internet before you start your letter. Or ask an adult to help you find the information.

ENVIRONMENTAL GROUPS

Many environmental groups offer information about water and how you can protect it. Here are just a few:

- **American Rivers**
  http://www.americanrivers.org/site/PageServer
  1101 14th Street NW, Suite 1400
  Washington, DC 20005
  202-347-7550

- **Blue Planet Project**
  http://www.blueplanetproject.net
  c/o The Council of Canadians
  170 Laurier Avenue W.
  Ottawa, ON K1P 5V5
  800-387-7177

- **Clean Water Fund**
  http://www.cleanwaterfund.org
  4455 Connecticut Avenue NW, Suite A300-16
  Washington, DC 20008
  202-895-0432

- **Waterkeeper Alliance**
  http://www.waterkeeper.org
  50 S. Buckhout, Suite 302
  Irvington, NY 10533
  914-674-0622

65

GLOSSARY

acid precipitation: rain, sleet, hail, or snow that falls from clouds polluted with acids

aquifer: a natural formation of sand, soil, gravel, or rock in which groundwater is collected and stored

bioaccumulation: the process by which human-made pollutants remain and accumulate in the bodies of animals

chlorination: a process in which chlorine is added to water to disinfect it

desalination: a process in which saline water, or salt water, is made into freshwater

dispersant: a chemical that breaks down oil and transforms it into a substance that is less harmful to aquatic life

ecosystem: a community of living things that depend on one another and their shared environment

environmentalism: a social movement that sees pollution as a preventable crime against nature

erosion: the gradual wearing away of soil

eutrophication: a process in which overaccumulation of nutrients, such as nitrogen and phosphorus, causes so much algae growth that water is deprived of oxygen

evaporation: the process of changing from a liquid into a gas

filtration: a process in which water is cleansed

gray water: the liquid drained from clothes washers, sinks, and showers. Gray water can be used in place of freshwater for many purposes, including watering lawns and plants.

groundwater: water that lies under Earth's surface

hypoxia: a deficiency of oxygen in water

irrigation: systems of waterways or sprayers for watering crops

pollutant: a substance that makes the land, air, or water dirty

precipitation: the name for water that falls from the sky. Precipitation can be rain, sleet, hail, or snow.

runoff: rain, sleet, hail, or snow that flows into bodies of water

sediment: soil, sand, and minerals that get into freshwater when runoff carries them into water bodies

sorbent: a spongy material that can soak up oil. Sorbents are used to clean up oil spills.

surface water: the water found in lakes, streams, rivers, and wetlands

toxin: poison

transpiration: a process in which plants release water into the air through tiny holes in their leaves

water cycle: the continuous movement of water from Earth's surface to the atmosphere and back again

watershed: an area of land that drains into a particular body of water

water system: an underground network of iron and plastic piping that delivers purified water to homes and businesses

water vapor: a gas that forms when liquid water evaporates

67

SOURCE NOTE

38   Doug Hollingsworth, quoted in Claudia Herrera Hudson, "Science Hero: Reef Ball Foundation," *Myhero.com*, April 15, 2006, http://www.myhero.com/ myhero/hero.asp?hero=Reef_Ball_Tech_2005 (January 31, 2008).

SELECTED BIBLIOGRAPHY

Carson, Rachel. *Silent Spring*. Boston: Houghton Mifflin Company, 1962.

Fridell, Ron. *Environmental Issues*. Tarrytown, NY: Marshall Cavendish Benchmark, 2006.

McNeill, J. R. *Something New under the Sun: An Environmental History of the Twentieth-Century World*. New York: W. W. Norton & Company, 2000.

Speth, James Gustave. *Red Sky at Morning: America and the Crisis of the Global Environment*. New Haven, CT: Yale University Press, 2004.

Starke, Linda, ed. *State of the World 2006*. New York: W. W. Norton & Company, 2006.

———. *Vital Signs: 2006-2007*. New York: W. W. Norton & Company, 2006.

FURTHER READING

Fridell, Ron. *Amphibians in Danger: A Worldwide Warning*. New York: Franklin Watts, 1999. Read this title to learn all about amphibians—amazing but endangered animals that often live in watery habitats.

The Groundwater Foundation Kids Corner
http://www.groundwater.org/kc/kc.html
This website features information on groundwater for students and their teachers.

68

Rapp, Valerie. *Protecting Earth's Air Quality*. Minneapolis: Lerner Publications Company, 2009. Find out why air quality is important and what you can do to preserve it.

Recyclezone
http://www.recyclezone.org.uk/home.aspx
Visit Recyclezone to learn all about the three Rs: reducing, reusing, and recycling.

Science News for Kids
http://www.sciencenewsforkids.org
This site features articles about many different science topics—including Earth and our environment.

Sheppard, Charles. *Coral Reefs*. Stillwater, MN: Voyageur Press, 2002. In this title, you'll learn more about coral reefs—a fascinating aquatic ecosystem.

Vogt, Gregory L. *The Hydrosphere: Agent of Change*. Minneapolis: Twenty-First Century Books, 2007. Vogt takes an in-depth look at the hydrosphere—the part of Earth that contains surface water, groundwater, and other water sources.

Water Where You Live
http://www.epa.gov/ow/states.html
This site allows you to click on any state to find out all about its streams, rivers, lakes, and beaches.

Wick, Walter. *A Drop of Water*. New York: Scholastic, 1997. This selection features informative text and remarkable photos of water. It also includes experiments you can try.

Woods, Michael, and Mary B. Woods. *Environmental Disasters*. Minneapolis: Lerner Publications Company, 2008. From oil spills to toxic pollution, environmental disasters take an enormous toll on Earth's land and water. Read about some of the world's worst disasters in this engaging book.

INDEX

71

ABOUT THE AUTHOR

Ron Fridell has written for radio, television, and newspapers. He has also written books about the Human Genome Project, including *Decoding Life: Unraveling the Mysteries of the Genome*. In addition to writing books, Fridell regularly visits libraries and schools to conduct workshops on nonfiction writing.

PHOTO ACKNOWLEDGMENTS

The images in this book are used with the permission of: © Photodisc/Getty Images, pp. 1 (background and title), 3 (bottom), 19; © iStockphoto.com/Milos Luzanin, pp. 1, 3 (top); NASA/JSC, pp. 4-5; Agricultural Research Service, USDA, p. 5; © John Warden/SuperStock, p. 7; © Todd Strand/Independent Picture Service, pp. 7 (inset), 47, 54, 55 (bottom), 60, 63; © iStockphoto.com/Stephen Sweet, p. 8 (top); © Rick Poley/Visuals Unlimited, pp. 8 (bottom), 17; © Dr. Stanley Flegler/Visuals Unlimited, p. 9 (left); © iStockphoto.com/Cathleen Clapper, p. 9 (right); © Bill Hauser/Independent Picture Service, p. 10; © Erik Schaffer; Ecoscene/CORBIS, p. 11; © iStockphoto.com/Midhat Becar, p. 12; © Royalty-Free/CORBIS, p. 13; © Inga Spence/Visuals Unlimited, p. 14; © Stockbyte/SuperStock, p. 16; © Daniel Dempster Photography/Alamy, p. 20; © Charlotte Thege/Alamy, p. 21; © iStockphoto.com/Jill Fromer, p. 22; © SuperStock, Inc./SuperStock, pp. 23, 26; © iStockphoto.com/Mark Evans, p. 24 (top); © John S. Lough/Visuals Unlimited, p. 24 (bottom); © iStockphoto.com/Pauline Mills, p. 27; © iStockphoto.com/Iurii Konoval, p. 28; © Bettmann/CORBIS, p. 29; © JH Pete Carmichael/The Image Bank/Getty Images, p. 31; Courtesy of Action for Nature, www.actionfornature.org, pp. 33, 52; AP Photo/C.J. Gunther, File, p. 35; © iStockphoto.com/Vyacheslav Anyakin, p. 36 (top); AP Photo/Rob Stapleton, p. 36 (bottom); AP Photo/Jack Smith, p. 37; © 2005 Jerry Kojansow & Reef Ball Foundation, www.reefball.org, p. 39; © Robert Ghemet/epa/CORBIS, p. 40; AP Photo/The Daily Sun, Terry Ketron, p. 43 (inset); © Alix Henry, p. 43; © iStockphoto.com/Leslie Banks, p. 44; © James Marshall/CORBIS, p. 45; © Hendrik Holler/Bon Appetit/Alamy, p. 46; © David M. Dennis/Animals Animals, p. 48; © Michael S. Lewis/CORBIS, p. 49; © age fotostock/SuperStock, p. 51; © Gianluigi Guercia/AFP/Getty Images, p. 53; © Daniel Staquet/Image Works/Time & Life Pictures/Getty Images, p. 55 (top); © Science Museum/SSPL/The Image Works, p. 57; © Don Emmert/AFP/Getty Images, p. 58; AP Photo/Barry Sweet, p. 61; © Peter Anderson/Dorling Kindersley/Getty Images, p. 62.

Front Cover: © Photodisc/Getty Images (background, title, and spine); © iStockphoto.com/Martin Strmko (top left); AP Photo/The News Tribune, Peter Haley (right); © iStockphoto.com/Milos Luzanin (bottom left). Back Cover: © Photodisc/Getty Images.